ANGEL REESE

BY KIM THOMPSON

AMICUS LEARNING

Inspire is published by
Amicus Learning, an imprint of Amicus
P.O. Box 227
Mankato, MN 56002
www.amicuspublishing.us

Copyright © 2025 Amicus.
International copyright reserved in all countries.
No part of this book may be reproduced in any form
without written permission from the publisher.

Editor: Ana Brauer
Series Designer: Kathleen Petelinsek
Book Designer: Rhea Magaro

Library of Congress Cataloging-in-Publication Data
Names: Thompson, Kim, 1970- author. | Reese, Angel, 2002-
Title: Angel Reese / by Kim Thompson.
Description: Mankato, MN : Amicus Learning, 2025. | Series: Inspire | Includes bibliographical references and index. | Audience: Ages 5-9 | Audience: Grades 2-3 | Summary: "Learn about WNBA star Angel Reese in an engaging biography packed with action photos and fact-filled text. Elementary sports fans will learn about Reese's childhood, her record-breaking college basketball career, and her rookie year with the Chicago Sky. Includes table of contents, glossary, further resources, and index"— Provided by publisher.
Identifiers: LCCN 2024035638 (print) | LCCN 2024035639 (ebook) | ISBN 9798892006316 (library binding) | ISBN 9798892006330 (paperback) | ISBN 9798892006354 (ebook)
Subjects: LCSH: Women basketball players—United States—Biography—Juvenile literature.
Classification: LCC GV884.R44 T56 2025 (print) | LCC GV884.R44 (ebook) | DDC 796.323092 [B]—dc23/eng/20240816
LC record available at https://lccn.loc.gov/2024035638
LC ebook record available at https://lccn.loc.gov/2024035639

Photo Credits: Alamy Stock Photo/Sports Press Photo, 5, SOPA Images, 11, Media Punch, 20; Associated Press/Reggie Hildred, 6, Julio Cortez, 10, Matthew Hinton, 12, Melissa Tamez/Icon Sportswire, 16-17, Ross D. Franklin, 18; Getty Images/Michael Reaves, 9, Kevin C. Cox, 13, C. Morgan Engel, 14; Icon Sportswire/Melissa Tamez, cover; Shutterstock/Naypong Studio, 7

Printed in the United States of America

Table of Contents

- 4 Double-Double
- 7 A Basketball Family
- 8 Top Recruit
- 11 Tough Times
- 12 A Terrific Tiger
- 15 Champs
- 16 Going Pro
- 19 All-Star
- 21 Style and Heart
- 22 Super Stats
- 23 Glossary
- 24 Read More
- 24 On the Web
- 24 Index

Double-Double

Angel Reese plays in the Women's National Basketball Association (WNBA). Her team is the Chicago Sky. The star is known for double-doubles. That means she gets double-digit scores in two areas like shooting, **rebounds**, or **assists**.

A LEADER
People look up to Reese. She speaks out about what is important to her. She wants to own a WNBA team.

Fans love it when Reese goes for a rebound.

Julian Reese plays for the University of Maryland.

A Basketball Family

Reese started playing basketball when she was four. Her mom and dad played on pro teams. Her cousin plays in the NBA. Her brother Julian is a college player. As kids, Angel and Julian shot baskets in their driveway.

TWO ANGELS
Angel and her mom share a first name. Angel used to watch "Big Angel" play basketball. She wanted to be like her.

Top Recruit

Reese led her high school team to three championships. Her school **retired** her jersey number. She was the number two college **recruit** in the country.

At 17, Reese played in the SLAM Summer Classic.

Reese worked hard to come back after she got hurt.

Tough Times

Reese went to the University of Maryland. She had some tough times. Some games were not held because of COVID-19. Reese broke her foot. She missed more games. She said, "I needed a fresh start."

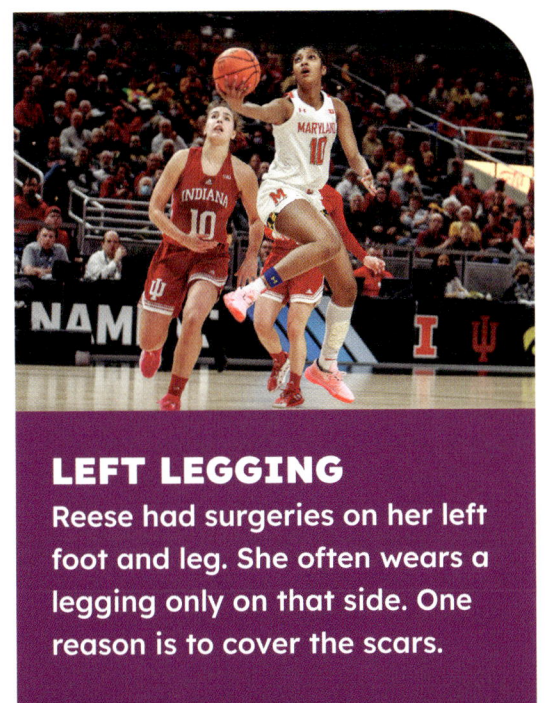

LEFT LEGGING
Reese had surgeries on her left foot and leg. She often wears a legging only on that side. One reason is to cover the scars.

A Terrific Tiger

Reese **transferred** to Louisiana State University. She grew close to coach Kim Mulkey. Reese was an LSU Tiger for two years. She scored more than 20 points per game. She got 34 double-doubles in one year. It set a league record.

FATHER FIGURE
At LSU, Reese met NBA legend Shaquille O'Neal. She says he is like a father to her.

Reese was the nation's top college rebounder.

Reese said, "Never let anyone tell you no or that you can't do this."

Champs

LSU played in the final game of the 2023 NCAA tournament. They beat the Iowa Hawkeyes 102 to 85. Reese scored 15 points. The Tigers were national champions! Reese was named Most Outstanding Player of the tournament.

HONORED
Reese was a First Team All-American in 2023. This is one of the highest honors for college players.

Going Pro

After college, Reese turned pro. She was one of the Chicago Sky's top picks. As a **rookie**, Reese broke WNBA records. She got double-doubles for 15 games in a row. She had 446 rebounds in one season.

All-Star Reese had 12 points and 11 rebounds.

All-Star

Reese was picked to play in the 2024 WNBA All-Star game. The game showed her talent for getting rebounds. Reese was the first rookie to get a double-double in the All-Star game.

Reese posed on the red carpet after winning an award.

Style and Heart

Reese likes to dress up. She likes to show her style. She runs the Angel C. Reese Foundation. The charity supports girls and women. It fights bullying. It helps people who have faced injustice.

SUPER STATS

ANGEL REESE

Born: May 6, 2002
Birthplace: Randallstown, Maryland
Current Team: Chicago Sky
Position: Forward

AWARDS

All-American, First Team: 2023
BET Sportswoman of the Year: 2023
ESPYS Award, Best Breakthrough Athlete: 2023
FIBA Women's AmeriCup, Silver Medalist: 2023
NCAA Champion: 2023
NCAA Final Four Most Outstanding Player: 2023
SEC Player of the Year: 2024
Wooden Award All-America Team: 2024

GLOSSARY

assist A pass of the ball to teammates that leads to scoring points.

rebound A time when a player gets a ball that someone from the other team shot and missed.

recruit A player who just became eligible to play in a league; a newcomer.

retire To stop using; to honor a player by not using their number for any future players.

rookie A player in their first year with the league.

transfer To move to a new school or a new team.

READ MORE

Bechtel, Mark. **"First Family: LSU's Angel Reese and UConn's Jordan Hawkins Are NCAA Champs and Cousins."** *Sports Illustrated for Kids*, May-June, 2023.

Chandler, Matt. **Basketball Biographies for Kids: The Greatest NBA and WNBA Players from the 1960s to Today.** New York: Callisto Kids, 2022.

Sports Illustrated Kids. **Big Book of WHO: Women in Sports.** New York: Sports Illustrated, 2024.

ON THE WEB

The Angel C. Reese Foundation
https://www.angelcreesefoundation.org/about

Chicago Sky
https://sky.wnba.com

WNBA – Angel Reese
https://www.wnba.com/player/1642291/angel-reese

INDEX

All-Star Team, WNBA, 19
championships, 8, 15
Chicago Sky, 4, 17
double-doubles, 4, 12, 17, 19
family, 6, 7
injury, 10, 11
legging 11
Louisiana State University, 12, 13
Mulkey, Kim, 12
O'Neal, Shaquille, 12
University of Maryland, 6, 10, 11
WNBA, 4, 17, 19

About the Author

Kim Thompson is a teacher and writer from Columbus, Ohio. She is a big basketball fan. She loves it when a close game gets exciting and the arena gets loud. She cheers and stomps her feet with the rest of the crowd.